eiring av nasjonaldagen 17. mai foran slottet.

Constitution Day (17. May) parade in front of
he Royal Palace.

AKER BRYGGE

AKERSHUS FESTNING
AKERSHUS CASTLE

OSLO havn - OSLO harbour

AKER BRYGGE

Christian Radich og Kongeskipet.

School ship Christian Radich and the Royal ship.

GRAHAM W. A. MACALLISTER
"PORTORA"
30 CARTSBRIDGE ROAD
BUSBY
GLASGOW G76 8DH
TEL. 0141 644 2260

CHRISTIAN IV

"Her skal byen ligge!"

"Here the town shall lie!"

"Hier soll die Stadt liegen!"

"La ville se situera ici!"

"Aquí se erguirá la Ciudad!"

NORWAY INFORMATION CENTER

OSLO Rådhus - OSLO Town Hall

Nye og gamle Rådhus
The new and the old Town Hall

OSLO Rådhus er bekjent for sin rike utsmykning utført av landets største kunstnere.

OSLO's Town Hall is renowned for the lavishness of its decorations, te work of Norway's greatest artists.

HAAKON VII
NORGES KONGE
1905 1957

Skulpturer av Ulf Aas foran Vikaterrassen
Statues by Ulf Aas in front of Vikaterrassen

NATIONALTEATRET

AKERSHUS FESTNING

Byens gamle Universitet fra 1811
The old University from 1811

Frihetsmonument ved
AKERSHUS FESTNING

Liberty monument at
AKERSHUS CASTLE

AKERSHUS FESTNING er et populært rekreasjons-
område for byens befolkning.

AKERSHUS CASTLE and surrounding parks are a
popular recuperation area for the Oslo citizens.

STORTINGET er Norges nasjonalforsamling. Her sitter 165 representanter som velges ved stortingsvalg hvert 4. år.

The STORTING, Norway's national assembly comprises 165 members. Elections are held every four years.

TEATERKAFEEN, et populært møtested i sentrum.
TEATERKAFEEN is a popular meeting point in Oslo city.

EIDSVOLDS PLASS - Karl Johans gate

OSLO DOMKIRKE

OSLO DOMKIRKE

STUDENTERLUNDEN mot slottet

PER GYNT
statue på Ankerbroen (Dyre Vaa).

PER GYNT statue by Dyre Vaa at Ankerbroen (Per Gynt is a famous character in one of Ibsens dramas).

ABELMONUMENTET foran Slottet
THE ABEL MONUMENT in front of the Royal Palace

KIRKERISTEN med salgsboder - KIRKERISTEN and old market place

Kongefamilien på Slottsbalkongen under feiring av nasjonaldagen 17. mai.

The Royal family at the balcony of the Royal Palace on Constitution Day (17. May).

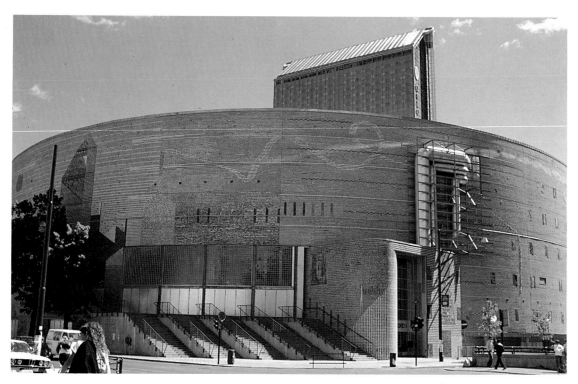

OSLO SPEKTRUM

OSLO PLAZA HOTEL

OSLO CENTRAL STATION

BLINDERN - den nye delen av Oslo universitetet
BLINDERN - the new part of Oslo University

Den gamle og
nye tid i Oslo

Ancient and modern
times in Oslo

SJØFARTSUMEEET, Bygdøy
THE MARITIME MUSEUM, Bygdøy

Slede fra Oseberg funnet
Sledge from the Oseberg
excarvation

Polarskipet FRAM   The Polar vessel FRAM

Balsaflåten Kon Tiki har fått sitt eget museum på Bygdøy. Thor Heyerdahl sammen med 5 mann seilte 8000 km med den fra Peru til Raroia på Polonesia i løpet av 101 døgn, fra 28. april til 7. august 1947.

Kon Tiki, Thor Heyerdahls balsa raft, is housed in a museum of its own on the Bygdø Peninsula. In the space of 101 days (28. April - 7. August 1947) Heyerdahl and five companions sailed this raft 8000 kilometres, crossing from Peru to Raroia in Polonesia.

OSEBERGSKIPET, Norges rikeste funn fra vikingtiden, ble gjort på Oseberg i Vestfold i 1904

The Oseberg ship, Norways finest relic of the Viking Age, was excarvated at Oseberg on the shores of the Oslo Fjord in 1904

VIGELANDSPARKEN

I sin skulpturpark på Frogner har Gustav Vigeland i bronse og sten skildret menneskets vandring fra vuggen til graven.

In the Sculpture Park at Frogner Gustav Vigeland has portrayed in stone and bronze mans progress from the cradle to the grave.

Ung mann og kvinne.
Marmor. 1906.

Young man and woman.
Marble. 1906.

Henrik Ibsens Portrett
i gips, 1903

Author Henrik Ibsens
Portrait in plaster, 1903

NORSK FOLKEMUSEUM på Bygdøy.
Foruten friluftsmuséet, råder muséet over
store samlinger av folkekunst og
bruksgjenstander.

THE NORWEGIAN FOLK MUSEUM at
Bygdøy possesses valuable collections of
folk art and handicrafts.

Stemmen 1893

Da vår største kunstner Edvard Munch døde i 1944, testamenterte han alle sine arbeider til Oslo kommune.

On his death in 1944, Edvard Munch, Norways greatest artist, left all his works to the Municipality of Oslo.

HOLMENKOLLEN, verdens mest
berømte vintersportsarena.

HOLMENKOLLEN SKI JUMP provides
the venue for the worlds major Ski meet.

HOLMENKOLLEN PARK HOTEL

I umiddelbar tilknytning til Holmenkollbakken, finner vi et moderne skimuseum som viser skisportens utvikling i Norge gjennom århundrer.

Adjacent the Holmenkollen Ski Jump there is a modern museum tracing the evolution of this national sport over the centuries.

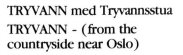
TRYVANN med Tryvannsstua
TRYVANN - (from the
countryside near Oslo)

Utsikt fra TRYVANNSTÅRNET

FROGNERSETEREN

KIKUT - et populært utfartssted i Oslomarka
KIKUT - a popular ski resort in the Oslo area.

BLANKVANNSBRÅTEN, Nordmarka   (from the countryside near Oslo)

The Oslo of today has evolved from a modest trading centre, founded round about 1048 at the head of the fjord of the same name, but as far back as the Iron Age there was a marketplace on the site, surrounded by a huddle of rude huts, boathouses, and other buildings. Time and again, however, the capital beneath the heights of Ekeberg was ravaged by fire, and after a last big blaze in 1624 King Christian IV resolved that it should be rebuilt on the other side of the Aker river, close to Akershus Castle. Renamed Christiania, the new town continued to prosper and expand, despite a series of setbacks that included war, fire, and pestilence. In 1811 it was honoured with a university of its own, and after dissolution of the union with Denmark in 1814 it automatically assumed the role of national administrative centre. In 1925 the town readopted its original name of Oslo. Present-day Oslo has a population of 450,000. Occupying the whole of the area around the inner reaches of the fjord, it is a modern city noted for its scenic location and superb natural surroundings.

The Royal Palace and the parliament building (Storting) are but two of Oslo's many attractions. The painter Edvard Munch bequeathed the bulk of his work to the city, which erected a special building, the Munch Museum, to house them.

The Kon-Tiki raft, on which Thor Heyerdahl crossed the Pacific in 1947, likewise occupies a museum of its own. Standing on the Bygdøy peninsula, just across the harbour, it is only a stone's throw from other notable relics of the past – the polar exploration vessel "Fram", two ninth-century Viking ships, and the Norwegian Folk Museum, a comprehensive collection of rustic buildings and folk art drawn from all over Norway.

Other major attractions include the Vigeland Sculpture Park and, in the hills above the city, the Holmenkollen Ski Jump.

今日のオスロは、町と同じ名前のフィヨルドの奥に1048年頃できた小さな交易所から発展してきたものですが、それよりずっと昔の鉄器時代にも同じ場所に交易所があり、そのまわりに粗末な家や舟小屋などがごちゃごちゃと建っていました。しかし、エーケベルグの下にあった町の中心は、何度か火事にあって荒廃し、1624年の大火災の後、クリスチャン四世はアーケル川の反対側のアーケル城塞の近くに町を再建することに決定しました。クリスチャニアと改名された新しい町は、戦争・火災・ペストなどによる挫折にもかかわらず、繁栄し拡大し続けました。1811年には独自の大学をもつ栄誉を受け、1814年のデンマークとの連合国家が分解した後には、この町は自然に国の行政の中心としての役割を担うことになりました。1925年には町の名が元のオスロに戻りました。

現在のオスロは45万の人口をもち、オスロ・フィヨルドの最奥部一帯を占め、風光に恵まれた位置にあり、素晴らしい自然に囲まれた近代都市です。

王宮と国会議事堂(Storting)の建物は、多くのオスロの見所のうちでも特記すべきものです。画家エドワルド・ムンクは彼の全作品を市に遺贈し、それらを収納するために特別な建物、ムンク美術館が建てられました。

1947年にトール・ハイエルダールが太平洋を横断した時の筏、コンチキ号もそのために建てられた博物館に保存されています。港の対岸の、石を投げれば届くほどの距離にあるビグドイ半島には、もう一つの過去の記念物、極地探検船のフラム号や、九世紀に造られた二隻のヴィキング船の博物館があり、また、ノルウェー民族博物館もあって、そこには全国から集められた田舎の建物や民族芸術品がまとめて展示されています。その外の主な見所としては、ヴィーゲラン彫刻公園と町の裏の丘の上にあるホルメンコーレン・スキージャンプ台などがあります。